2050: A Vision of Tomorrow's World

By Divyan Gupta

First Edition
March 2023

Dedication

This book is dedicated to my family

CONTENTS

Introduction

The world of 2050 may seem like a distant reality, but in rapidly changing landscape driven by technological advancements, it is closer than we think. "**2050: A Vision of Tomorrow's World**" aims to explore the possibilities of our world in the coming decades, offering readers a thought-provoking journey through a time of unparalleled transformation.

This book will delve into various aspects of our future, including demographic shifts, technological advancements like AI and Robotics, economic paradigms, societal changes, education and work and others that impact all of us. As we traverse through these topics, we will encounter a world that is both exciting and, at times, daunting. We will witness the potential for both utopia and dystopia, as well as the inherent responsibility we have as a global society to shape our future. "**2050: A Vision of Tomorrow's World**" is not a mere projection of trends, nor is it an attempt to predict the future with certainty. Rather, it is an invitation to engage with the possibilities that lie ahead and to reflect on the choices we must make today in order to create the world we want for ourselves and future generations.

DEMOGRAPHIC SHIFTS

In the world of 2050, demographic shifts will reshape the global landscape, giving rise to new opportunities and challenges. As we venture into the future, it is essential that we understand these transformations and their implications for society, economy, and geopolitics. In this section, we will delve into the major demographic trends that will define our world in the coming decades.

Population Growth and Decline

By 2050, the global population is expected to reach 9.7 billion, up from 7.8 billion in 2021. However, this growth will not be evenly distributed. While some regions, particularly Africa and parts of Asia, will experience significant population growth, others, including Europe and East Asia, will face a declining population. This divergence will create a new set of challenges for countries experiencing rapid population growth, such as increased pressure on resources, infrastructure, and social systems. On the other hand, nations with shrinking populations will need to confront the issues of an aging population, economic stagnation, and potential labor shortages.

Aging Population

As life expectancy continues to rise and birth rates decline, the world will witness a significant increase in the proportion of elderly individuals. By 2050, it is estimated that more than 20% of the global population will be aged 60 or older, compared to 13%
in 2021. An aging population will have profound implications for healthcare systems, pensions, and social security, as well as the labor market. Nations will need to develop innovative strategies to address these challenges, such as embracing new technologies, rethinking retirement policies, and promoting lifelong learning and reskilling.

Urbanization

By 2050, around 68% of the global population is projected to live in urban areas, up from 55% in 2018. Rapid urbanization will give rise to mega-cities, with several cities exceeding 10 million inhabitants. This concentration of people and resources will create both opportunities and challenges, as cities become the focal points of innovation, economic growth, and social change.

Managing this urban growth will require significant investments in infrastructure, housing, and public services to ensure that cities remain livable, sustainable, and resilient. Furthermore, the rise of smart cities, leveraging data and technology to improve urban life, will become an essential part of the urban landscape in 2050.

Migration and Multiculturalism

In an increasingly interconnected world, the movement of people across borders will continue to shape societies and economies. Migration, driven by factors such as economic opportunity,
conflict, and climate change, will contribute to the diversification of communities and the spread of ideas and innovation.

The growing multiculturalism will bring both benefits and challenges, as societies grapple with issues of integration, identity, and social cohesion. Developing policies that promote inclusivity, tolerance, and the equitable distribution of resources will be essential in fostering harmonious and diverse societies.

The Youth Bulge

In regions experiencing rapid population growth, a significant proportion of the population will be young. This youth bulge presents a unique opportunity for nations to harness the potential of their young population, investing in education and skills development to drive economic growth and innovation.

However, if not managed effectively, the youth bulge could exacerbate unemployment, social unrest, and political instability. As such, it is crucial that governments prioritize youth empowerment and create opportunities for their meaningful engagement in society.

In conclusion, the demographic shifts of 2050 will reshape the world in profound ways, offering both challenges and opportunities. By understanding and proactively addressing these trends, we can work together to build a more equitable, prosperous, and inclusive global community.

TECHNOLOGICAL ADVANCEMENTS

The world of 2050 will be shaped by ground breaking technological advancements that have the potential to revolutionize various aspects of our lives. In this section, we will explore some of the key technologies that will define our future, along with their potential implications and challenges.

Artificial Intelligence and Robotics

Artificial Intelligence (AI) and robotics will permeate nearly every industry and aspect of our lives, leading to significant improvements in efficiency, productivity, and problem-solving capabilities. From self-driving cars and smart homes to AI-powered medical diagnostics and personalized education, these technologies will transform the way we live, work, and interact. Let's examine some of the areas where AI and Automation will have a major impact.

1. AI and Automation in the Workforce

The increasing capabilities of AI and automation technologies will lead to a significant transformation of the labour market, with some jobs disappearing while new ones emerge.

This shift will necessitate a focus on workforce adaptability, skills development, and the creation of social safety nets to support workers through periods of transition.

Furthermore, addressing the ethical and economic implications of AI-driven unemployment and wealth disparities will be critical to ensure that the benefits of these technologies are equitably distributed and do not exacerbate existing inequalities.

2. AI and the Future of Decision-Making

AI has the potential to revolutionize the way we make decisions, from everyday choices to high stakes matters in areas such as finance, healthcare, and government policy. By processing vast amounts of data and identifying patterns, AI can provide insights and recommendations that improve efficiency, accuracy, and outcomes.

However, the increasing reliance on AI in decision-making also raises concerns about accountability, transparency, and potential biases embedded in algorithms. Addressing these issues will require the development of ethical guidelines, regulatory frameworks, and AI auditing mechanisms that ensure the responsible and fair use of AI in decision-making processes.

3. AI and Creative Industries

As AI technologies become more sophisticated, they will increasingly be used in creative industries such as art, music, and literature, generating new forms of artistic expression and challenging our understanding of creativity and authorship. This will raise questions about intellectual property rights, the value of human creativity, and the potential for AI-generated content to blur the lines between reality and fiction.

Navigating these complexities will require a re-evaluation of our cultural and legal frameworks, as well as a deeper understanding of the relationship between humans and AI in the creative process.

4. AI and Personalized Experiences

AI will play a significant role in shaping our daily experiences, from personalized recommendations and targeted advertising to customized healthcare and education. By tailoring products and services to individual preferences, AI can enhance convenience, efficiency, and satisfaction.

At the same time, the increasing personalization of experiences raises concerns about privacy, surveillance, and the potential for manipulation. Addressing these challenges will require robust data protection regulations, as well as a commitment to ethical AI design and implementation.

5. AI and Global Governance

AI will play an increasingly important role in global governance, as countries and international organizations turn to these technologies to address complex challenges such as climate change, public health, and cybersecurity. AI can facilitate international collaboration, data sharing, and decision-making, helping to tackle pressing global issues more effectively and efficiently.

However, the growing influence of AI in global governance also highlights the need for international agreements and frameworks that govern the development, deployment, and the use of AI technologies, ensuring that they are harnessed for the collective benefit of humanity.

In conclusion, the future of AI in 2050 will be shaped by our ability to navigate the numerous ethical, legal, and social challenges that these technologies present, as well as our willingness to collaborate and share knowledge in pursuit of the greater good. Ensuring that AI and robotics benefit humanity as a whole will require thoughtful regulation, collaboration, and a focus on human-centred design. By embracing the transformative potential of AI while remaining vigilant to its risks, we can ensure that this powerful technology serves as a force for progress for all humanity.

Biotechnology and Health

In 2050, biotechnology will revolutionize healthcare, enabling personalized medicine, advanced gene therapies, and the potential to eradicate genetic diseases. Developments in genomics, synthetic biology, and regenerative medicine will lead to novel treatments for a range of conditions, extending lifespans and improving overall health.

While these advancements offer tremendous potential, they also raise ethical and moral questions about genetic engineering, human enhancement, and the equitable distribution of these technologies. Balancing innovation with responsible governance will be crucial in ensuring that the benefits of biotechnology reach all members of society.

Human Augmentation and Enhancement

As we move towards 2050, the boundaries between humans and technology will continue to blur, as advancements in fields such as biotechnology, neuroscience, and nanotechnology enable us to augment and enhance our physical and cognitive capabilities.

It will be necessary to study the potential impact of human augmentation and enhancement on society and the challenges that will arise as we redefine the limits of human potential.

1. Physical Augmentation and Wearable Technologies

Developments in wearable technologies, prosthetics, and exoskeletons will enable us to augment our physical abilities, improving strength, endurance, and sensory perception. These advancements will have significant implications for various domains, including healthcare, sports, and the military, as well as for individuals with disabilities.

However, the widespread adoption of physical augmentation technologies will also raise ethical and social concerns, such as the potential for unequal access to these enhancements and the implications for human identity and self-perception.

2. Cognitive Enhancement and Brain-Computer Interfaces

Advances in neuroscience and brain-computer interfaces (BCIs) will enable us to enhance our cognitive abilities, including memory, attention, and problem-solving skills. This will have profound implications for education, work, and our everyday lives, as we become more efficient, adaptable, and intelligent.

At the same time, the prospect of cognitive enhancement raises questions about the potential risks to mental health, privacy, and autonomy, as well as the ethical implications of altering our natural cognitive abilities.

3. Genetic Engineering and Designer Babies

As our understanding of genetics advances, the prospect of using technologies such as CRISPR to edit human genes and design our offspring becomes increasingly feasible. This could enable us to eradicate genetic diseases, enhance physical and cognitive abilities, and even extend our lifespans.

However, the prospect of genetic engineering raises significant ethical, social, and legal concerns, including the potential for eugenics, the commodification of human life, and the exacerbation of existing inequalities.

4. The Ethics of Human Augmentation and Enhancement

As human augmentation and enhancement technologies become more widespread, it will be essential to address the ethical and social implications of these advancements. This will involve grappling with questions related to human dignity, identity, and the limits of our desire to improve ourselves.

In addition, fostering public dialogue, developing regulatory frameworks, and ensuring equal access to these technologies will be critical in ensuring that the benefits of human augmentation and enhancement are shared equitably and responsibly.

5. The Impact of Augmentation and Enhancement on Society

The widespread adoption of human augmentation and enhancement technologies has the potential to significantly impact society, as we redefine our understanding of what it means to be human. This will require us to rethink our social, cultural, and legal frameworks, as well as address the potential for increased inequality and the erosion of our shared sense of humanity.

In conclusion, the future of human augmentation and enhancement in 2050 will be shaped by our ability to navigate the complex ethical, legal, and social challenges that these advancements present, as well as our commitment to ensuring that the benefits of these technologies are harnessed for the greater good of humanity. By doing so, we can ensure that human augmentation and enhancement serve as a powerful catalyst for progress and human flourishing, while also preserving our shared values and sense of identity.

Space Exploration

The next decades will witness a new era of space exploration, with both government agencies and private companies pushing the boundaries of what is possible. From the establishment of lunar bases and manned missions to Mars to the commercialization of space travel and the exploitation of extra-terrestrial resources, space will become an increasingly important domain for human activity and provide an exciting and transformative frontier.

These advancements in space exploration will have far-reaching implications for our understanding of the universe, technological innovation, and international cooperation. However, they will also present new challenges, such as space debris management, the militarization of space, and the need for clear regulations to govern activities beyond Earth.

1. Commercial Space Travel and Tourism

The rise of commercial space travel, spearheaded by companies such as SpaceX, Blue Origin, and Virgin Galactic, will democratize access to space and open up new opportunities for tourism, research, and industry. As the cost of space travel decreases and the technology becomes more accessible, space tourism will transition from a niche pursuit for the wealthy to a more mainstream experience.

However, the growth of commercial space travel will also raise questions related to regulation, safety, and environmental impacts, necessitating a coordinated and responsible approach to space tourism and its associated industries.

2. Space-Based Industries and Resource Extraction

The exploitation of space-based resources, such as minerals from asteroids and water from the lunar surface, will become an increasingly important driver of space exploration and colonization. The development of space-based industries will create new economic opportunities and technological innovations, as well as help to reduce the cost and complexity of space missions.

At the same time, the extraction and utilization of space resources will pose challenges related to governance, property rights, and the potential for conflict, requiring the establishment of international norms and agreements to ensure the responsible and equitable use of these resources.

3. Human Settlements on the Moon and Mars

One of the most ambitious goals of space exploration in the coming decades will be the establishment of human settlements on the Moon and Mars. These endeavours will not only serve as stepping stones for further exploration of the solar system but also provide valuable insights into the challenges and opportunities of long-term human habitation in space.

Achieving this goal will require significant advancements in areas such as life support systems, radiation protection, and in-situ resource utilization, as well as international collaboration and a shared commitment to the peaceful and cooperative exploration of space.

4. Space Science and the Search for Extraterrestrial Life

The search for extraterrestrial life and the study of the cosmos will continue to be major drivers of space exploration, as we seek to answer fundamental questions about the origins and nature of life in the universe. Advances in astronomy, astrobiology, and planetary science will enable us to explore distant planets and celestial bodies, while new observatories and missions will push the boundaries of our knowledge and understanding.

In addition, the discovery of extraterrestrial life, whether microbial or more complex, would have profound implications for our understanding of ourselves and our place in the cosmos, with the potential to redefine the very nature of human existence.

5. International Cooperation and Space Governance

As space exploration and colonization become more prevalent, the need for international cooperation and effective governance will become increasingly important. This will involve establishing norms, treaties, and regulatory frameworks that address issues such as space debris, resource extraction, and the militarization of space, as well as fostering collaboration and trust among nations and other stakeholders.

In conclusion, the future of space exploration and colonization in 2050 will be shaped by our ability to harness technological innovations, forge international partnerships, and address the myriad ethical, legal, and environmental challenges that arise as we venture into the final frontier. By doing so, we can ensure that our journey into space not only advances human knowledge and progress but also fosters a deeper sense of global unity and shared purpose.

Renewable Energy and Climate Change Solutions

The world of 2050 will demand innovative solutions to address the pressing issue of climate change. Renewable energy technologies, such as solar, wind, and geothermal power, will play a critical role in reducing global carbon emissions and transitioning to a more sustainable energy future.

Moreover, breakthroughs in energy storage, carbon capture, and climate engineering will offer new ways to mitigate and adapt to the impacts of climate change. These developments will require substantial investments, international cooperation, and a global commitment to sustainability and environmental stewardship.

In summary, the technological advancements of 2050 promise to reshape our world in ways both thrilling and challenging. By embracing these innovations and addressing their potential risks and ethical concerns, we can harness the power of technology to create a brighter, more equitable, and sustainable future.

ECONOMIC PARADIGMS

As we venture into the world of 2050, the global economy will undergo significant transformations, driven by demographic shifts, technological advancements, and emerging markets. In this section, we will explore the key economic trends and paradigms that will define the future of our global economic landscape.

The Rise of Emerging Markets

By 2050, emerging markets, particularly in Asia and Africa, will become increasingly influential players in the global economy. Countries such as China, India, and Indonesia are projected to experience significant economic growth, leading to a shift in the balance of economic power from the West to the East.

This rise of emerging markets will create new opportunities for trade, investment, and innovation, while also presenting challenges related to competition, resource allocation, and global governance. Navigating these dynamics will require increased cooperation, diplomacy, and a commitment to multilateralism.

The Knowledge Economy

The future economy will be increasingly driven by knowledge, innovation, and intellectual capital, as industries shift towards high-value, technology-intensive sectors. This transition to a knowledge economy will place a premium on skills, education, and research and development, with countries and companies alike competing for top talent and cutting-edge innovation.

In this environment, fostering a culture of lifelong learning, creativity, and collaboration will be essential in ensuring a thriving, resilient, and inclusive economy that benefits all members of society.

The Circular Economy and Sustainable Development

The world of 2050 will require a fundamental shift in our approach to economic development, as we transition from a linear, resource-intensive model to a more sustainable, circular economy. This new paradigm will prioritize the efficient use of resources, waste reduction, and the regeneration of natural systems, aligning economic growth with environmental sustainability.

Achieving this vision will necessitate new business models, policy frameworks, and consumer behaviours that support sustainable production and consumption, as well as the development and adoption of clean technologies and green infrastructure.

The Gig Economy and Future of Work

Technological advancements, changing demographics, and evolving societal norms will reshape the nature of work in the coming decades. The gig economy, characterized by flexible, short-term, and project-based employment, will become an increasingly prominent feature of the labour market.

While this shift will provide new opportunities for autonomy, entrepreneurship, and work-life balance, it will also raise concerns related to job security, social safety nets, and worker rights. Adapting to this new landscape will require innovative approaches to social protection, labour regulations, and education and training.

Global Trade and Economic Cooperation

In a world that is increasingly interconnected and interdependent, global trade and economic cooperation will be vital in promoting prosperity, stability, and innovation. However, the future of trade will also be shaped by challenges such as protectionism, digital divides, and geopolitical tensions.

Addressing these challenges and fostering an open, rules-based global trading system will require renewed commitments to multilateralism, inclusive growth, and the equitable distribution of the benefits of trade and investment.

In conclusion, the economic paradigms of 2050 offer both opportunities and challenges, as we navigate a rapidly changing global landscape. By embracing these transformations and working together to build a more equitable, sustainable, and inclusive global economy, we can ensure that the world of 2050 is one of shared prosperity and opportunity for all.

SOCIETAL TRANSFORMATIONS

As we look ahead to the world of 2050, we will witness profound societal transformations, influenced by demographic shifts, technological advancements, and evolving cultural norms. In this section, we will explore the key social trends and issues that will shape our future societies.

The Digital Divide

As technology becomes an ever more integral part of our lives, addressing the digital divide will be critical in ensuring equal access to information, services, and opportunities. Bridging this gap will require investments in infrastructure, digital literacy, and affordable access to technology, particularly in underprivileged communities and developing nations.

In addition, addressing the digital divide will involve fostering digital inclusivity and combatting online discrimination, harassment, and misinformation, to create a safe and equitable digital environment for all.

Social Inequality and Inclusive Growth

In a world of increasing wealth and prosperity, addressing social inequality will be essential in ensuring that the benefits of economic growth are shared equitably among all members of society. This will involve tackling issues such as income disparities, wealth concentration, and unequal access to education, healthcare, and other resources.

Promoting inclusive growth will require a combination of progressive policies, social safety nets, and targeted investments in human capital and infrastructure, particularly in marginalized communities and developing nations.

Gender Equality and Women's Empowerment

Achieving gender equality and empowering women and girls will be a key priority in the world of 2050. This will involve addressing persistent gender gaps in education, health, economic opportunity, and political representation, as well as combatting gender-based violence and discrimination.

Empowering women and girls will not only promote social justice and human rights, but also unleash the potential of half of the world's population, contributing to economic growth, innovation, and global progress.

Cultural Identity and Globalization

As the world becomes more interconnected and diverse, fostering a sense of cultural identity and belonging will become increasingly important. This will involve embracing multiculturalism, promoting intercultural dialogue, and celebrating the richness of our diverse cultural heritage.

At the same time, globalization will continue to blur the lines between traditional cultural boundaries, giving rise to new forms of expression, collaboration, and identity. Navigating this complex interplay of cultures will require tolerance, empathy, and a commitment to mutual understanding and respect.

In conclusion, the societal transformations of 2050 will offer both challenges and opportunities, as we strive to create a more inclusive, equitable, and resilient global community.

By embracing these changes and working together to address the social issues of our time, we can build a brighter future for everyone.

ENVIRONMENTAL STEWARDSHIP

As we envision the world of 2050, safeguarding our planet's ecosystems and natural resources will be of paramount importance. In this section, we will explore the key environmental challenges and the strategies required to ensure a sustainable future for generations to come.

Climate Change Mitigation and Adaptation

Addressing climate change will be a defining challenge of the 21st century, requiring concerted global efforts to reduce greenhouse gas emissions and transition to low-carbon economies. This will involve investing in renewable energy, promoting energy efficiency, and developing innovative technologies for carbon capture and storage.

In addition to mitigation efforts, adapting to the impacts of climate change will be crucial, particularly for vulnerable communities and ecosystems. This will require strategies for climate-resilient infrastructure, disaster risk reduction, and ecosystem-based adaptation, among others.

Biodiversity Conservation

The preservation of Earth's biodiversity will be a critical priority in the coming decades, as we confront habitat loss, pollution, and climate change. This will involve protecting and restoring vital ecosystems, such as forests, wetlands, and coral reefs, as well as implementing sustainable land-use practices and promoting the sustainable use of natural resources.

Conserving biodiversity will also require addressing the illegal wildlife trade, invasive species, and other drivers of species loss, as well as fostering a greater appreciation for the intrinsic value of nature and the vital services it provides.

Water Security

As the global population grows and the demand for water increases, ensuring water security for all will be an essential challenge. This will involve improving water efficiency, promoting the sustainable use of water resources, and investing in infrastructure for water supply, sanitation, and waste management.

Furthermore, addressing water security will require innovative solutions for water management, such as the use of smart technologies, the recycling of wastewater, and the desalination of seawater, as well as enhanced cooperation and governance at local, regional, and global levels.

Sustainable Food Systems

Feeding a growing global population in a sustainable and equitable manner will be a key priority in the world of 2050. This will involve transforming our food systems to promote sustainable agricultural practices, reduce food waste, and enhance food security and nutrition.

Innovative approaches, such as vertical farming, precision agriculture, and alternative protein sources, will play a crucial role in creating more resilient and resource-efficient food systems. Additionally, fostering a global culture of responsible consumption and dietary choices will be essential in ensuring a sustainable food future.

Environmental Governance and Global Cooperation

Tackling the environmental challenges of 2050 will demand robust governance frameworks and international cooperation. This will involve strengthening existing environmental laws, policies, and institutions, as well as forging new agreements and partnerships to address emerging issues.

Crucially, environmental stewardship must be grounded in the principles of equity, justice, and intergenerational responsibility, ensuring that the needs of both present and future generations are met while safeguarding the health and integrity of our planet.

In conclusion, the world of 2050 will be defined by our collective commitment to environmental stewardship and our ability to adapt to and mitigate the impacts of environmental change. By working together to address these challenges, we can ensure a more sustainable, resilient, and thriving planet for generations to come.

THE FUTURE OF EDUCATION AND LEARNING

Education will play a pivotal role in shaping the world of 2050, as we prepare future generations to navigate the complex challenges and opportunities of an interconnected and rapidly evolving global landscape. In this section, we will explore the key trends and innovations that will redefine the future of education.

Personalized Learning and Adaptive Technologies

Advances in artificial intelligence, data analytics, and learning sciences will enable the development of personalized and adaptive learning experiences, tailored to individual needs, interests, and learning styles with real-time feedback.

While these innovations hold great promise, it will be essential to ensure that access to these cutting-edge technologies is equitable and inclusive, to avoid exacerbating existing educational disparities.

Competency-Based and Project-Based Learning

As the needs of the workforce and society continue to evolve, there will be an increasing emphasis on competency-based and project-based learning, which prioritize the development of skills and real-world applications over traditional content knowledge. This shift will require a re-evaluation of assessment and accreditation systems, as well as the development of new models for curriculum design and delivery.

Lifelong Learning and Skills Development

In a world characterized by rapid change and uncertainty, the importance of lifelong learning and continuous skills development will only grow. To thrive in the knowledge economy and adapt to evolving workforce demands, individuals will need to cultivate a growth mind set and embrace a culture of continuous learning and upskilling.

This will necessitate a shift in our approach to education, with greater emphasis on skills such as critical thinking, creativity, collaboration, and emotional intelligence, as well as flexible learning opportunities and innovative models for skills development and retraining.

Online and Blended Learning

The future of education will be increasingly characterized by a blend of online and traditional face-to-face learning, offering greater flexibility, accessibility, and diversity in educational experiences. Online platforms and digital resources will enable learners to access content and expertise from around the world, breaking down geographical barriers and fostering global collaboration.

However, the rise of online and blended learning will also present challenges related to digital equity, pedagogy, and student engagement. Ensuring the quality and inclusivity of these learning experiences will require investments in infrastructure, teacher training, and research on effective online pedagogies.

The Role of Teachers and the Learning Environment

In the world of 2050, the role of teachers will continue to evolve, as they transition from being the primary source of knowledge to facilitators of learning and mentors who guide and inspire students. This will involve embracing new pedagogies, technologies, and professional development opportunities, as well as cultivating a culture of innovation and collaboration within the teaching profession.

Moreover, the learning environment itself will be transformed, with a focus on creating flexible, inclusive, and engaging spaces that foster creativity, well-being, and a sense of community.

The Integration of Technology in the Classroom

The use of digital technologies in the classroom will continue to expand, as educators incorporate tools such as virtual reality, augmented reality, and gamification to create immersive and engaging learning experiences. These technologies have the potential to revolutionize the way we teach and learn, fostering collaboration, creativity, and critical thinking.

However, addressing the digital divide and ensuring equitable access to these technologies will be essential to avoid exacerbating existing inequalities in education.

The Globalization of Education

As the world becomes more interconnected, the globalization of education will continue to gain momentum. This will involve increased international collaboration in research, the development of globally recognized qualifications and credentials, and the growth of study abroad and international exchange programs. This will not only enhance the quality of education but also promote cultural understanding, empathy, and global citizenship.

While the globalization of education presents opportunities for cross-cultural learning and the exchange of ideas, it will also require addressing issues such as access, quality at a global scale, cultural sensitivity, and the equitable distribution of educational resources and opportunities.

The future of education and lifelong learning in 2050 will be shaped by our ability to harness the power of technology, adapt to the changing needs of society, and embrace a vision of learning that is inclusive, equitable, and focused on the holistic development of individuals. By doing so, we can ensure that education serves as a powerful tool for personal growth, social progress, and global understanding.

WORK AND EMPLOYMENT

As we look ahead to the world of 2050, the future of work and employment will be shaped by a multitude of factors, including technological advancements, demographic shifts, and evolving economic and social landscapes. In this section, we will explore the key trends and challenges that will define the labour market of the future.

Automation and Artificial Intelligence

Advances in automation and artificial intelligence (AI) will continue to disrupt traditional industries and job roles, as machines increasingly perform tasks that were once the domain of humans. This will lead to significant shifts in the labour market, with some jobs becoming obsolete while new ones emerge in response to the changing technological landscape.

Preparing for this future will require a focus on skills development and workforce adaptability, as well as policies and social safety nets that support workers through periods of transition and displacement.

The Gig Economy and New Forms of Employment

The rise of the gig economy and the proliferation of remote work, freelancing, and other flexible employment models will continue to reshape the way we work and the nature of employer-employee relationships. These new forms of employment offer opportunities for increased autonomy, flexibility, and entrepreneurship, but also present challenges related to job security, income stability, and access to social protections.

Addressing these challenges will require innovative approaches to labour regulation, social insurance, and worker representation, ensuring that the rights and well-being of all workers are protected, regardless of their employment status.

Skills Mismatch and the Future of Education

As the labour market evolves, addressing the skills mismatch between the education system and the needs of employers will be a critical challenge. This will involve fostering closer collaboration between educational institutions, industry, and government, as well as embracing new models of learning that prioritize lifelong skills development, adaptability, and the cultivation of in-demand competencies.

In addition, promoting equal access to quality education and training opportunities will be essential in ensuring that all individuals have the chance to succeed in the future labour market, regardless of their background or circumstances.

Demographic Shifts and the Intergenerational Workforce

As populations' age and life expectancies increase, the workforce of 2050 will be characterized by greater intergenerational diversity, with multiple generations working side by side. This will present both opportunities and challenges, as organizations and societies grapple with issues such as age discrimination, knowledge transfer, and the evolving nature of retirement.

Fostering a culture of intergenerational collaboration, learning, and mutual respect will be crucial in ensuring that the unique strengths and perspectives of each generation are harnessed for the benefit of all.

Globalization and the Future of Work

The continued globalization of the economy will have significant implications for the future of work, as industries and labour markets become increasingly interconnected and interdependent. This will create opportunities for global talent mobility, collaboration, and innovation, but also raise concerns related to job displacement, wage stagnation, and the offshoring of employment.

Navigating this complex landscape will require a commitment to fair and inclusive global labour practices, as well as coordinated efforts to address the social, economic, and political dimensions of globalization.

In conclusion, the future of work and employment in 2050 will be shaped by our ability to anticipate, adapt to, and navigate the myriad challenges and opportunities presented by technological, demographic, and global forces. By fostering a culture of learning, innovation, and resilience, we can ensure that the labour market of the future is one that supports the well-being and prosperity of all.

URBANIZATION AND SMART CITIES

By 2050, the majority of the world's population will be living in urban areas, making the future of urbanization and infrastructure a critical area of focus. In this section, we will explore the key trends and innovations that will shape the cities of the future and the infrastructure that supports them.

Smart Cities and the Internet of Things

The integration of technology in urban planning and management will give rise to smart cities, characterized by interconnected networks of sensors, devices, and systems that optimize the efficiency, sustainability, and livability of urban spaces. The Internet of Things (IoT) will enable real-time monitoring and data-driven decision-making, transforming areas such as transportation, energy management, and public safety.

While the potential benefits of smart cities are immense, it will be crucial to address issues related to privacy, security, and digital equity, ensuring that these technologies are used responsibly and inclusively.

Sustainable Urban Design and Green Infrastructure

As cities continue to expand, sustainable urban design and green infrastructure will become increasingly important in mitigating the environmental impacts of urbanization and promoting the well-being of urban residents. This will involve strategies such as compact city planning, mixed-use development, and the creation of green spaces, as well as the integration of renewable energy, waste management, and water conservation systems.

Furthermore, fostering a culture of sustainable consumption and lifestyle choices will be essential in ensuring the long-term viability of our urban ecosystems.

Housing and Affordability

Ensuring access to safe, affordable, and adequate housing will be a central challenge for the cities of the future, as urban populations continue to grow and housing markets evolve. Addressing this issue will require a combination of policy interventions, innovative financing models, and new approaches to housing design and construction.

Moreover, fostering inclusive communities and addressing issues of social segregation and gentrification will be essential in creating diverse, vibrant, and resilient urban neighbourhoods.

Urban Resilience and Disaster Risk Reduction

As cities face increasing risks from climate change, natural disasters, and other hazards, building urban resilience will become a critical priority. This will involve enhancing the capacity of cities to anticipate, adapt to, and recover from shocks and stresses, through strategies such as climate-resilient infrastructure, early warning systems, and community-based disaster risk reduction.

In conclusion, the cities of 2050 will be defined by our ability to balance the demands of urban growth with the need for sustainable, equitable, and resilient urban environments. By embracing innovation, collaboration, and forward-thinking urban planning, we can ensure that our cities remain vibrant and livable spaces for generations to come.

TRANSFORMATION OF TRANSPORTATION AND MOBILITY

In 2050, the world of transportation and mobility will undergo significant transformations, driven by technological innovations, environmental concerns, and shifting patterns of human behaviour. In this section, we will explore the key trends and developments that will shape the future of transportation and mobility in the coming decades.

The Rise of Autonomous Vehicles

The widespread adoption of autonomous vehicles will revolutionize the way we move, with self-driving cars, trucks, and buses becoming an integral part of our transportation systems. This will have significant implications for traffic management, urban planning, and public transportation, as well as for the automotive industry and job market.

However, the transition to autonomous vehicles will also present challenges related to safety, regulation, and infrastructure, as well as ethical considerations surrounding decision-making algorithms and the potential for job displacement.

Electric and Alternative Fuel Vehicles

The shift towards electric and alternative fuel vehicles will continue to accelerate, driven by concerns about climate change and the need to reduce our reliance on fossil fuels. This will lead to the development of more efficient batteries, charging infrastructure, and innovative transportation solutions, such as hydrogen fuel cell vehicles.

Addressing the environmental impact of transportation and ensuring the responsible and sustainable use of resources will be essential in shaping the future of mobility.

Integrated and Multimodal Transportation Systems

The future of transportation will be characterized by the integration of multiple modes of transport, as cities and regions adopt more comprehensive and user-friendly transportation networks. This will involve the development of smart infrastructure and the incorporation of new technologies, such as autonomous vehicles, drones, and Hyperloop systems.

Efforts to promote public transportation, cycling, and walking will also be crucial in reducing congestion, improving air quality, and enhancing the livability of our urban environments.

The Future of Air Travel and Space Tourism

Advancements in aerospace technology will lead to the development of more efficient and sustainable aircraft, as well as the emergence of new forms of air travel, such as supersonic and hypersonic flight. The prospect of commercial space tourism will also become increasingly feasible, with companies like SpaceX and Blue Origin developing reusable rocket technology and offering suborbital flights to private passengers.

Navigating the regulatory, environmental, and safety challenges associated with these new forms of air and space travel will be critical in shaping the future of transportation and mobility.

The Impact of Transportation Technologies on Society

The evolution of transportation technologies will have far-reaching implications for society, as we redefine the way we move, work, and live. Addressing issues such as accessibility, affordability, and the potential for job displacement will be essential in ensuring that the benefits of these advancements are equitably distributed.

Furthermore, fostering a culture of innovation and collaboration between the public and private sectors, as well as international cooperation, will be crucial in shaping the future of transportation and mobility in a way that promotes sustainability, equity, and human wellbeing.

In conclusion, the future of transportation and mobility in 2050 will be defined by our ability to adapt to new technologies, address the environmental and social challenges that they present, and harness their potential for improving the quality of life for people around the world. By embracing a holistic and forward-thinking approach to transportation and mobility, we can ensure a future that is efficient, sustainable, and accessible for all.

HEALTH AND WELL-BEING

In the world of 2050, advances in medical science, technology, and public health will continue to revolutionize our understanding of health and well-being. In this section, we will explore the key trends and innovations that will shape the future of healthcare and the ways in which we care for our physical and mental well-being.

Personalized Medicine and Precision Health

The rise of genomics, biotechnology, and big data analytics will usher in a new era of personalized medicine and precision health. This will involve tailoring medical treatments and interventions to an individual's unique genetic, environmental, and lifestyle factors, resulting in more effective and targeted therapies.

In addition to improving patient outcomes, personalized medicine has the potential to transform healthcare systems by enhancing prevention, early detection, and disease management, ultimately reducing the burden of chronic conditions and the associated costs.

Digital Health and Telemedicine

The integration of digital technologies in healthcare will continue to reshape the way we access, deliver, and manage health services. Telemedicine, wearable devices, and mobile health applications will enable remote monitoring, diagnosis, and treatment, breaking down barriers to healthcare access and empowering individuals to take greater control of their health.

As digital health technologies become more widespread, it will be essential to address issues related to data privacy, security, and the digital divide, ensuring that these innovations are used responsibly and equitably.

Mental Health and Emotional Well-being

In the coming decades, mental health and well-being will become increasingly important as we confront the challenges and opportunities of a rapidly changing world. Issues such as stress, anxiety, depression, and addiction will require innovative approaches to prevention, treatment, and support.

As our understanding of the importance of mental health and emotional well-being continues to grow, there will be an increasing emphasis on holistic approaches that recognizes the interconnectedness of physical, mental, and social health, as well as the importance of community, resilience, and self-care. This will involve promoting mental health awareness, destigmatizing mental illness, and integrating mental health services into primary care settings.

Furthermore, advances in neuroscience, psychology, and digital technologies will give rise to new therapies and interventions for mental health conditions, as well as innovative tools for promoting emotional well-being and resilience.

Aging and Longevity

As life expectancies increase and populations age, addressing the health and well-being of older adults will become a central focus of healthcare in the coming decades. This will involve promoting healthy aging through preventive strategies, as well as developing new treatments and care models for age-related diseases, such as Alzheimer's, Parkinson's, and age-related macular degeneration.

In addition, fostering intergenerational connections and addressing the social determinants of health will be essential in ensuring that older adults can age with dignity, purpose, and a strong sense of community.

Global Health and Health Equity

In the world of 2050, addressing global health disparities and promoting health equity will be critical challenges. This will involve strengthening healthcare systems and infrastructure in low- and middle-income countries, as well as addressing the social, economic, and environmental factors that contribute to health inequities.

Collaboration and solidarity among nations, communities, and individuals will be vital in tackling these complex challenges and ensuring that the benefits of healthcare innovations and advancements are shared equitably among all people.

In conclusion, the future of health and well-being in 2050 will be shaped by our collective efforts to embrace innovation, promote equity, and foster a holistic understanding of health that encompasses both the physical and mental dimensions of well-being. By working together to address these challenges, we can create a healthier, happier, and more resilient world for generations to come.

EVOLUTION OF WARFARE

The nature of warfare is poised to undergo significant changes by 2050, driven by technological advancements and shifts in geopolitical power dynamics. While the threat of war remains a constant, how we engage in conflict will be fundamentally different.

Autonomous Weapons Systems

The increasing sophistication of AI and robotics will lead to the development of autonomous weapons systems. These machines, capable of making independent decisions on the battlefield, will alter the nature of warfare, raising ethical and legal questions about the role of humans in conflict.

Cyber Warfare

Cyber warfare will become a prominent aspect of conflict, with nations investing heavily in their cyber capabilities. Attacks on critical infrastructure, such as power grids and communication networks, will become more frequent and sophisticated, with the potential to cripple entire nations.

Space Warfare

The militarization of space will emerge as a new frontier in warfare, with nations racing to secure their interests in Earth's orbit and beyond. Satellite systems will become prime targets, as they play an increasingly vital role in communication, surveillance, and navigation.

Biotechnology and Warfare

Advances in biotechnology will lead to new forms of biological and chemical weapons, with the potential for targeted attacks on specific populations or ecosystems. This will necessitate the development of novel defense strategies and countermeasures.

Non-state Actors

The rise of non-state actors, such as terrorist organizations and criminal networks, will challenge traditional notions of warfare. These groups will increasingly leverage advanced technologies, such as drones and AI, to engage in asymmetric warfare against nation-states.

Hybrid Warfare

The blending of conventional and unconventional warfare techniques will become more prevalent, as nations engage in hybrid warfare to achieve their objectives. This includes the use of information warfare, propaganda, and covert operations to influence public opinion and destabilize adversaries.

Hyper-connected Battlefield

The Internet of Things (IoT) and the widespread adoption of digital communication technologies will create a hyper-connected battlefield, where vast amounts of data are collected and analyzed in real-time. This will enable new levels of situational awareness and decision-making, as well as the potential for vulnerabilities that can be exploited by adversaries.

Ethical and Legal Challenges

The changing nature of warfare will present new ethical and legal challenges, as nations grapple with questions surrounding the use of autonomous weapons, cyber warfare, and the militarization of space. International laws and treaties will need to evolve to address these emerging issues.

Human Enhancement

Advances in biotechnology, neuroscience, and materials science will pave the way for human enhancement technologies, which could be used to create "super soldiers" with increased physical and cognitive abilities. This raises ethical questions about the use of such technologies and their potential impact on the nature of warfare and society at large.

New Alliances and Power Dynamics

As the geopolitical landscape shifts and new technologies emerge, alliances and power dynamics will evolve, creating new tensions and opportunities for conflict. Ensuring stability and preventing escalation will require increased cooperation and diplomacy among nations.

The future of warfare will be shaped by these and other factors, as humanity navigates an increasingly complex and interconnected world.

It is crucial that we engage in open dialogue about the implications of these changes and work together to create a future that prioritizes peace, stability, and global cooperation.

GLOBAL COOPERATION AND CHALLENGES

In the lead-up to 2050, the world will face numerous global challenges that will require unprecedented levels of cooperation, understanding, and collective action. In this section, we will explore the key issues and potential areas of collaboration that will shape the future of global cooperation and our ability to confront these pressing challenges.

Climate Change and Environmental Preservation

Addressing climate change and preserving the environment will be among the most critical global challenges of the coming decades. Tackling this issue will necessitate international collaboration in the areas of emissions reduction, renewable energy development, and environmental conservation.

Countries will need to work together to develop and implement comprehensive climate policies, share technological innovations, and provide financial and technical support to vulnerable nations. In doing so, we can foster a global culture of environmental stewardship and promote a sustainable future for all.

Poverty Alleviation and Economic Inequality

Reducing poverty and addressing economic inequality will be essential in promoting social stability and sustainable development across the globe. This will involve fostering international cooperation in areas such as trade, investment, education, healthcare, and infrastructure development.

By working together to create inclusive economic systems, promote fair labour practices, and ensure access to resources and opportunities for all, countries can build a more equitable and prosperous world.

Global Health and Pandemic Preparedness

The COVID-19 pandemic has highlighted the need for international collaboration and preparedness in the face of global health threats. In the coming decades, countries will need to work together to strengthen public health systems, invest in medical research, and develop strategies for the prevention and management of infectious diseases.

By fostering a global culture of health security and resilience, we can ensure that the world is better equipped to confront future pandemics and health crises.

Cybersecurity and the Digital Domain

As our reliance on digital technologies continues to grow, so too will the need for international cooperation in the area of cybersecurity. Countries will need to collaborate on the development and implementation of cybersecurity frameworks, share threat intelligence, and invest in the protection of critical infrastructure and information systems.

Addressing the challenges posed by cyber threats will be essential in safeguarding the digital domain and ensuring the stability and security of our interconnected world.

Peace, Security, and Disarmament

In an increasingly complex and interconnected world, fostering global peace, security, and disarmament will be more critical than ever.

This will involve promoting diplomacy and dialogue, addressing the root causes of conflict, and working towards the reduction and eventual elimination of weapons of mass destruction.

By embracing a cooperative and inclusive approach to global security, we can build a more peaceful and stable world for future generations.

In conclusion, the future of global cooperation and our ability to confront the challenges of 2050 will depend on our commitment to international collaboration, empathy, and shared responsibility. By embracing these values and working together to address the pressing issues facing our planet, we can create a more just, sustainable, and peaceful world for all.

THE ROAD AHEAD

The road ahead to 2050 is filled with both promise and uncertainty. The decisions we make today and the actions we take as a global community will have a profound impact on the future of our planet and the lives of generations to come. In this section, we will explore the potential pathways and strategies for navigating the challenges and opportunities that lie ahead.

Embracing Innovation and Technological Progress

The future will be shaped by our ability to harness the power of innovation and technological progress, as we seek to address the complex and interconnected challenges facing our world. By fostering a culture of curiosity, creativity, and collaboration, we can ensure that the advancements of the coming decades are utilized for the benefit of all.

At the same time, we must remain vigilant about the ethical, social, and environmental implications of new technologies, and work together to develop responsible and inclusive frameworks for their use and regulation.

Fostering Inclusive and Sustainable Development

As the global population continues to grow and the demands on our planet's resources intensify, promoting inclusive and sustainable development will be more critical than ever. This will involve rethinking our economic models, prioritizing social equity and environmental stewardship, and adopting innovative solutions to complex challenges such as climate change, poverty, and resource scarcity.

By embracing a holistic and forward-thinking approach to development, we can ensure a future that is prosperous, resilient, and equitable for all.

Strengthening Global Governance and Cooperation

The road ahead will require unprecedented levels of global governance and cooperation, as we confront the challenges and opportunities of an increasingly interconnected world. By strengthening international institutions, promoting diplomacy and dialogue, and fostering a culture of shared responsibility, we can build a more just, peaceful, and collaborative world.

Investing in Education and Human Capital

The future will be defined by the knowledge, skills, and capabilities of our global population. By investing in education and human capital, we can empower individuals and communities to adapt to the changing world, contribute to the development of innovative solutions, and drive progress towards a more sustainable, equitable, and prosperous future.

Cultivating Empathy, Understanding, and Global Citizenship

Lastly, the road ahead will demand a new era of empathy, understanding, and global citizenship, as we seek to bridge the divides that separate us and build a more inclusive and interconnected world. By fostering cross-cultural dialogue, embracing diversity, and nurturing a sense of shared humanity, we can create a future that is defined by unity, compassion, and mutual respect.

In conclusion, the road to 2050 is filled with both challenges and opportunities, and the choices we make today will shape the world for generations to come.

By embracing a spirit of innovation, cooperation, and empathy, we can navigate the complexities of the future and create a world that is more just, sustainable, and prosperous for all.

In conclusion, as we stand at the precipice of a new era, the world of 2050 holds immense potential for growth, transformation, and progress. The path we choose to follow will be determined by our collective courage, wisdom, and determination to forge a better future for ourselves and the generations to come. In the face of unprecedented challenges and opportunities, our success will be measured by our ability to adapt, collaborate, and uphold the values of empathy, sustainability, and inclusivity.

The journey to 2050 will not be without its hurdles, and the responsibility falls upon each one of us to embrace change, engage in meaningful dialogue, and strive to make informed decisions that prioritize the greater good. Our collective actions will shape the course of history, and our legacy will be defined by the world we leave behind for our children and grandchildren.

Let this book serve as both a guide and an inspiration, a call to action and a reminder of the power that lies within each of us to make a difference. As we navigate the complexities of the coming decades, may we do so with a spirit of curiosity, resilience, and optimism, guided by the knowledge that our greatest challenges can also be our most profound opportunities for growth and transformation.

In the words of the renowned anthropologist Margaret Mead, "Never doubt that a small group of thoughtful, committed citizens can change the world; indeed, it's the only thing that ever has." As we embark on this journey towards 2050, let us carry this message in our hearts and minds, remembering that the power to shape the future resides within each of us, and that together, we can create a world that is more just, sustainable, and prosperous for all.

The world of 2050 awaits. Let us rise to the challenge, embrace our shared destiny, and write the next chapter of human history with courage, compassion, and hope.

ABOUT THE AUTHOR

Divyan Gupta is a futurist, strategy and management expert, and an author with an academic background in political science and management. As a sought-after consultant, advisor and speaker, Divyan is recognized for his ability to simplify complex concepts and present them in a captivating manner.

Divyan brings a unique perspective to understanding global trends and the future of human society. He has devoted more than 20 years to researching and analyzing the interplay of technology, politics, and business, establishing himself as a thought leader in envisioning the world of tomorrow.

Divyan has been covered in both print and electronic media. His expertise covers a broad spectrum of topics, including innovation, geopolitics, management and organizational strategy.

In his consulting capacity, Divyan has advised numerous corporations, start-ups and government agencies, helping them develop innovative strategies to tackle the challenges of the 21st century. His insights have guided decision-makers in fields such as entrepreneurship, policy making, economic development, and governance.

As an author, Divyan's work is driven by his passion for understanding the intricate relationships that define our global society and his commitment to promoting a more sustainable and just future for all.

When not traveling the world to share his knowledge or attending conferences, Divyan enjoys immersing himself in the world of knowledge or exploring the hidden corners of our planet with his family. He is an enthusiastic supporter of community building especially those focusing on entrepreneurship, culture and arts.

To connect with him, simply scan the QR code below.

www.ingramcontent.com/pod-product-compliance
Lightning Source LLC
Chambersburg PA
CBHW062112160726
48282CB00026B/769
9789358913026